#ApoemAday

Tweet poetry

vol. #2

William Forchion

Dreamcatcher Entertainment, LLC

Brattleboro, VT 05301
www.dreamcatcherfilmworks.com

cover photo: Vincent Cotnoir © 2016
cover design: Dreamcatcher Entertainment, LLC
© 2018

ISBN-13: 978-0-9982978-3-5
ISBN-10: 0-9982978-3-6

To: JLS

For the beautiful flower that blossomed unexpectedly in my heart.

I will flood the world with words if it is the way to have you float through my life again.
Only the kindest most loving words I would use, for they are the only words capable of buoying you here.

Introduction

During the month of April, national poetry month I began writing a poem a day, first thing in the morning, then posting them on twitter. Regularly I would share the day's poem with my mother during our morning phone call. I had tasked myself to make it through the month writing a poem a day. As the month concluded I decided to continue writing and tweeting. I did not give myself an end date yet knew that I would take all poems written up to June 30th and publish them. On June 30th my mother died unexpectedly. In honor of my mother, my biggest fan and best friend, I publish this second installment. Also in honor of my mother I will continue to write a poem a day for a complete year. This is the second installment.

July 1

Dear mom, long and Short has been you
hair, through it all I knew you'd care, when I
lost hope in a God above, it was through
your loving I restored my love, you are no
longer here my dear, yet I know you are
everywhere.

#ApoemAday #lovingmom #IAmEnough
#Billosophy #greiving

July 2

Must I wake? I can only find you in the
dream, longing, to hold you, and hear
you, like just the other day, you've gone,
I will find you when I close my eyes.

#ApoemAday #poetry #IAmEnough
#Billosophy #iloveumom

July 3

The world has shattered, reeling from
explosion, awash in pain, standing at
the epicenter, amidst the debri of the
entirety of existence, fuzzy, yellow,
unsure, a new universe to explore.

#ApoemAday #poetry #amwriting
#Billosophy #4Eva

July 4

Sally forth, celebrate, set fire to the
sky, independence, let loose, a joyful
cry, together, apart, radiate joy, heart
full, peace, spirit dance, soul song,
wing away in burdenless flight, love.

#ApoemAday #poetry #IAmEnough
#Billosophy #amwriting #4Eva

July 5

a veil of clouds, the rain does fall,
blue sky remains beyond it all.

#ApoemAday #IAmEnough #poetry
#Billosophy #4Eva

July 6

Mirror image, reality altered, the life
reflected, living the opposite of the
life projected, each conflicted about
existence after crossing the
meridian.

July 7

Change remains constant,
inspiration, expiration, transition,
from death to birth and back,
persistent evolution, the cycle of
love, the process of living.

#ApoemAday #IAmEnough #poetry
#amwriting #Billosophy #4Eva

July 8

A day like any other, fresh start, new
possibilities, filled with silences and
sounds, laughter and love,
potentials, room for growth and
wisdom, today.

#ApoemAday #IAmEnough #poetry
#Billosophy #4Eva

July 9

Pour myself into the new, similarities
abound, fresh start, flowing in the
direction of time, an abundance of
miracles stacked neatly awaiting
distribution, boundless possibilities,
today.

#ApoemAday #IAmEnough #poetry
#Billosophy #amwriting #4Eva

July 10

The flower opens with the sun and
closes with the moon, the tree
unfurls leaves with the warmth and
sheds with the cold, the human
learns with day and dreams with the
night, the cycle from young to old.

#ApoemAday #IAmEnough #poetry
#Billosophy #4Eva

July 11

Transition, transfer, evolution, the greater portion of life is lived in between stations, enroute to our destination.

#ApoemAday #IAmEnough #poetry #amwriting #Billosophy #4Eva

July 12

Rapidly the earth spins beneath my feet, honor bound I move in synchrony with ground, uncertain the destination, I focus on the journey, discovering a new self with each stride.

#ApoemAday #IAmEnough #poetry #Billosophy #amwriting #4Eva

July 13

With each breath the intoxicating
elixir of life drips down the back of
my throat soaking into my soul in a
welcomed way like a strongly
needed blessing.

#ApoemAday #IAmEnough #poetry
#Billosophy #amwriting #4Eva

July 14

Chance meeting, in you resonates a
familiar, a glimmer, near recognition,
common words spoken, shared
incantations, uncanny similarities,
squinting, I know you, deep down,
inside.

July 15

Egg cracked on the horizon, yolk
rising, casting light onto a new day,
hatching infinite possibilities.

#ApoemAday #Billosophy #poetry
#IAmEnough #amwriting #4Eva

July 16

Light in darkness, is not always cast
from above, as the rainfall, snowfall ,
sunny day, neither a good or bad, all
perspective shifts, filtered in love.

#ApoemAday #IAmEnough #poetry
#Billosophy #amwriting #4Eva

July 17

Vast uncharted territory,
undiscovered imaginings, love and
joy generation to unfathomable
capacity, wisdom and unknowing
co-habitting, within the depths of the
mind.

#ApoemAday #IAmEnough #poetry
#Billosophy #amwriting #4Eva

July 18

Walls crumble, glass breaks, tears
roll down the face, there is
separation, the happenings around
me, the happenings within me, may
influence yet are not me, by grace.

#ApoemAday #IAmEnough #poetry
#amwriting #Billosophy #4Eva

July 19

I pour into me, soul nourishing
content, beauty, kindness,
knowledge, friendship, love, too
often I am force fed, soul sapping
substances, I know when i show the
world what I need, the divine will
ensure I feed.

July 20

drip to drop on I go, over around and
through, mountains, trees and rocks,
on I flow, ever changing from
moment to moment, ever the same
for an eternity, i am the river,
powerful and calm at once,
constantly limitless.

#ApoemAday #IAmEnough #poetry
#Billosophy #amwriting #4Eva

July 21

night cedes to day, the cabinet of
possibilities is flung open,
somewhere rain, somewhere snow,
somewhere cotton dotted sky, life
kisses life, time reveals new secrets,
Love happens.

#ApoemAday #IAmEnough #poetry
#Billosophy #4Eva #amwriting

July 22

Blessings rain down like water from the sky, put away the umbrella, put away the raincoat, bathe in the divine gifts, shower in love.

#ApoemADay #IAmEnough #poetry #Billosophy #amwriting #gardensofEva

July 23

Walking, though fully asleep, reality
warping, wrapping around itself, to
conjure itself anew, inverted
understanding creating wonder filled
existence.

#ApoemAday #IAmEnough #poetry
#Billosophy #amwriting
#gardensofEva

July 24

Perched at the edge, dive in to
discover? Soar above to see?
Validation of each choice is the
living. Pondering, retreating, valid
too, each choice a solution, as the
living story writes itself in the living.

July 25

Flowing freely, day by day, night and day, an estuary of divine love, a constant ever changing current, of spirit for the world, unseen, omnipresent, power filled, pure, tireless, without end, flowing freely.

#ApoemAday #IAmEnough #poetry
#Billosophy #gardensofEva
#amwriting

July 26

Ever changing, undulating, ever
present, pulsing, soothing at times,
energizing when necessary, dancing
to the rhythm of life.

#ApoemAday #IAmEnough #poetry
#Billosophy #amwriting
#gardensofEva

July 27

For just a moment, set aside
anticipation, imagination,
assumption, to take in what is, for
what is without what if, removes
frustration, allowing what is to be
what is.

#ApoemAday #IAmEnough #poetry
#Billosophy #amwriting
#gardensofEva

July 28

One day is not defined by, one
stumble, one mistake, one life is
defined by, the love it gives, the joy it
makes.

July 29

Wake up, the goddess within, wake
up, the miracle maker, ask the ego to
go on vacation, the godly side,
inside, suffers under ego's watch, let
the sun rise inside, ask the divine to
take over, now shine, shine, shine.

#ApoemAday #IAmEnough #poetry
#Billosophy #gardensofEva

July 30

The divine pours into, the vessel,
me, chipped, cracked, broken, the
love of divinity restores, if I allow.

#ApoemAday #IAmEnough #poetry
#Billosophy #amwriting
#gardensofEva

July 31

Within the embers smolder, feeding
on life fuel, a gentle breeze temping,
enticed by opportunity, imagination,
sparked by the divine, nourish the
fire, the task is mine.

#ApoemAday #poetry #IAmEnough
#Billosophy #amwriting
#gardensofEva

Aug. 1

In the comforting stillness, there is
nothing to fear, nestled in a fog bank
of love, the quiet contains the
answer, divine calm, peace.

#ApoemAday #IAmEnough #poetry
#Billosophy #amwriting
#gardensofEva

Aug. 2

Morning settles upon my head like a
pigeon vying for attention, not subtly
straining, waking me to what is, a
new day, shoo bird, there are things
to do.

#ApoemAday #IAmEnough #poetry
#Billosophy #amwriting
#gardensofEva

Aug. 3

Hearts break and mend, clouds
form, rain falls, sun shines, living is
an equitable mixture, and hopefully
lovingly unbalanced.

#ApoemAday #IAmEnough #poetry
#Billosophy #amwriting
#gardensofEva

Aug. 4

Trapped with limitless possibilities,
the soul purposefully seeks, release
from the body, return to the divine,
fulfilling wholeness.

#ApoemAday #IAmEnough #poetry
#Billosophy #amwriting
#gardensofEva

Aug. 5

For the briefest moment, our paths
crossed, time became irrelevant, half
became whole, fear dissipated as
Love saturated all, in the void of your
absence, hope is encouraged, until
our paths cross again.

#ApoemAday #IAmEnough #poetry
#Billosophy #gardensofEva
#amwriting

Aug. 6

Shattered vessel, pieces scattered,
wholeness in hindsight, all is illusion,
oneness is many pieces lovingly
joined, seeing only the pieces is to
overlook the divine, for without love
the vessel is only pieces.

#ApoemAday #IAmEnough #poetry
#Billosophy #amwriting
#gardensofEva

Aug. 7

In the burbling stream, the song of
life is spoken, the trees echo the
words, all others join the chorus, I
listen and add my voice.

#ApoemAday #IAmEnough #poetry
#Billosophy #amwriting
#gardensofEva

Aug. 8

Step by step rising to new
awareness, overcoming the stares of
life, precariously perched between
falling and flying, floating in the
wonderment of living.

#ApoemAday #IAmEnough
#Billosophy #poetry #writing
#gardensofEva

Aug. 9

an inky vastness with beings of
brilliance positioned in perfection,
unknowable to all but one, we hold
the night within the stars, that light
created leaves doubt without
shadow, as we dream within the
dream.

#ApoemAday #IAmEnough #poetry
#amwriting #Billosophy
#gardensofEva

Aug. 10

Each breathe a recycled wash of
wisdom and imagination, inspiration
seeking form, knowledge searching
for an interpreter to transform air into
creation, forming the living words of
the divine.

#ApoemAday #IAmEnough #poetry
#Billosophy #amwriting
#gardensofEva

Aug. 11

Waking within the dream, dreaming while awake, two faces of the same coin, straddling the chasm of awareness, succumbing to the infinite, surrendering to the divine, becoming fully alive.

#ApoemAday #IAmEnough #poetry #Billosophy #amwriting #gardensofEva

Aug. 12

The answers and the questions
tumble together, life is not a puzzle
to be solved, it is an adventure to be
lived, in discovery of an answer and
a question and a silly side note.

#ApoemAday #IAmEnough #poetry
#Billosophy #amwriting
#gardensofEva

Aug. 13

Like the water in the stream, the
words flow, not always
understandable, often wrapped in
multiple meanings, cascading into
the world, resonating forever.

#ApoemAday #IAmEnough #poetry
#Billosophy #amwriting
#gardensofEva

Aug. 14

Flying, soaring, effort transforming
into effortlessness, as complex and
wonderful as dreaming a miraculous
life into being, and possible,
definitely possible.

#ApoemAday #IAmEnough #poetry
#Billosophy #amwriting
#gardensofEva

Aug. 15

Air thickens in the lungs, imagination
becomes fear, all becomes work, as
the dreamer awakens, the dream
remains awaiting the dreamers
return.

#ApoemAday #IAmEnough #poetry
#Billosophy #amwriting
#gardensofEva

Aug. 16

Just for a moment, it all stops,
nothing matters, no consequences,
everything seen anew, without
opinion,the burden of life lifted,
revealing the levity of living, alive
unencumbered, Love is all that is,
just for a moment.

#ApoemAday #IAmEnough #poetry
#Billosophy #gardensofEva

Aug. 17

I am the rain, washing away all that
is not you, activating the fertilizer of
growth, creating space among all,
filling the void, welcome and
unwanted, universal essence of life, I
am the rain.

#ApoemAday #IAmEnough #poetry
#Billosophy #amwriting
#gardensofEva

Aug. 18

I am wind, neutral, at peace, ably
amassing gale force, gently flickering
a candle flame, toppling tree as a
cyclone, delicately carrying
orchestral nuance as a summer
breeze, lovingly, I am wind.

#ApoemAday #IAmEnough #poetry
#Billosophy #amwriting
#gardensofEva

Aug. 19

I am earth, an independent piece of
the universe, galactic, molecular,
living host, provider, non-judgmental,
consistently ever changing, mother,
father, baby, adrift, eternally alone, I
am earth.

#ApoemAday #IAmEnough #poetry
#Billosophy #amwriting
#gardensofEva

Aug. 20

I am fire, soul warming, dancing,
breathing, sustainer, consumer,
consistently unpredictable, curious,
playful, mesmerizing to almost
magical, powerful, I am fire.

#ApoemAday #IAmEnough #poetry
#Billosophy #gardensofEva

Aug. 21

The sun rises over easy on a new
day, a new me, fresh possibilities
hatch to be discovered and
nourished, shadows diminish as the
daylight washes clean the darkness,
illuminating the present.

#ApoemAday #IAmEnough #poetry
#amwriting #Billosophy
#gardensofEva

Aug. 22

Outside becomes inside, the
contents and the container morph
into one while remaining
independent, a transformation of
perspective without loss of identity,
each moment of each day, and then,
flight.

Aug. 23

Rising from the toes, from the heart, from the soul, an unwritten song with never a sour note, to be sung solo or in chorus, unique in each iteration, cathartic, cleansing, rejuvenating, a laugh.

#ApoemAday #IAmEnough #poetry #amwriting #Billosophy #gardensofEva

Aug. 24

I lay aside anger frustration and fear,
moving on without looking back,
load lightened without these
persistent passengers, I journey on
discovering a new world, a new me.

#ApoemAday #IAmEnough #poetry
#amwriting #Billosophy
#gardensofEva

Aug. 25

I know happiness, joy, sorrow,
sadness, frustration, love, my
questions and answers are many
and unpaired, a magical amazing life
I am living, and grateful I am for
another solar lap.

#ApoemAday #IAmEnough #poetry
#amwriting #Billosophy
#gardensofEva

Aug. 26

Create, time stands still, create, pour
life through self into the unknown,
create, un-crate a package divinely
ordered, create, a fragment of the
answer of the question of life, create,
the heartbeat of universal being.

#ApoemAday #IAmEnough #poetry
#Billosophy #gardensofEva

Aug. 27

Fragile to a fault, give in, allow the
me that I know to crumble, explode,
fragment, never again to be whole,
new, changed forever, strong beyond
belief, timeless, limitless,
transcendent being of light and love.

#ApoemAday #IAmEnough #poetry
#Billosophy #amwriting
#gardensofEva

Aug. 27

Looking without seeing,
living without loving,
being without dreaming, now open,
experience, breathe, share,
create beauty, we have the choice to
live fully.

#IAmEnough Billosophy
#gardensofEva

Aug. 28

It happened, when I stopped trusting
me, my ego took over, lies became
truth when I believed hard enough,
and spirit an illusion for those who
think too much, I killed God.

Aug. 29

In the space between the letters of
the smallest word, in the silence that
surrounds the smallest sound, in the
moment between breathes and
heartbeats, dwells an infinite divine
everything.

#ApoemAday #IAmEnough #poetry
#Billosophy #amwriting
#gardensofEva

Aug. 30

Trapped, partly heaven, partly hell,
walls unseen impenetrable by force,
all consuming nothingness, filled to
overflowing with everything,
entrance and exit illogically paired,
oasis, prison, my mind.

#ApoemAday #IAmEnough #poetry
#Billosophy #amwriting
#gardensofEva

Aug. 31

The universe reached down and
plucked me up, I wept, sobbed,
aware of the pain I carried as I was
bathed in love and joy, safe to
wonder, safe to see, without the
baggage, who I will be.

#ApoemAday #IAmEnough #poetry
#amwriting #Billosophy
#gardensofEva

Sept. 1

The war rages on, battlements
fortified, fear, love, head, heart, gut,
sometimes allies, sometimes
advisories, mind body spirit dis-
joined, the soul the prize to the
victor.

#ApoenAday #IAmEnough #poetry
#amwriting #Billosophy
#gardensofEva

Sept. 2

Within the eye of the storm, calm,
devastation a potential, dissipation
also possible, centered, sheltered,
protected by and from immeasurable
power, grace.

#ApoemADay #IAmEnough #poetry
#Billosophy #amwriting
#gardensofEva

Sept. 3

Eyes gently close, entering the new
world, discovering a new self,
inverted not mirrored, inspiration and
expiration reversed, un-living a new
life, half awake, half asleep, fully
alive.

#ApoemAday #IAmEnough #poetry
#amwriting #Billosophy
#gardensofEva

Sept. 4

Freeze time, in what moment? Joy,
sorrow, ecstasy, frivolity, the moment
stretched rebounds to erasure, lived
once and never lived again, unfreeze
time, remember, live now.

#ApoemAday #IAmEnough #poetry
#amwriting #Billosophy
#gardensofEva

Sept. 5

Morning fog, neither cloud nor mist,
existing in space, without sinking or
rising, my mind clears, my feet rise
off the ground, I become the
morning fog awaiting evaporation in
the warmth of the sun.

#ApoemAday #IAmEnough #poetry
#amwriting #Billosophy
#gardensofEva

Sept. 6

Adrift on cosmic winds, pollen,
dander, engaged in pursuit of the
closure of the circuit, validation in
potential, catalyst of transformation,
driven with divine purpose.

#ApoemAday #IAmEnough #poetry
#amwriting #Billosophy
#gardensofEva

Sept. 7

Fresh, morning dew, gentle touch,
the puff of wind coaxing the hairs of
the arm to bow, silent, a loving
thought memory wafting awake in
the mind, perfect.

#ApoemAday #IAmEnough #poetry
#amwriting #Billosophy
#gardensofEva

Sept. 8

Give in to gravity, fall into the loving
embrace of eternity, release fault fear
shame, what remains is the
confident capable gift from the
divine, our birthright, strength power
love, trust, love me anew.

Sept. 9

This moment, the unknowable is known, the present is unwrapped, wake up fresh, born again, new, perfect, a day that has never been begins.

#ApoemAday #IAmEnough #poetry #amwriting #Billosophy #gardensofEva

Sept. 10

Morning chill, color muted, clouds cool blanket the suns warmth, seasonal change, a sneeze hovers on the horizon, dew settles on the field tempted to be frost, life slows, a reflection of the past foretelling the future.

Sept. 11

Throb throb, throb brain rages
against bone, threatening to
explode, pain, pain beyond pain, lie
down, no respite, throb, ache,
heartbeat, ache, migraine induced
insanity, clarity in reverse.

#ApoemAday #IAmEnough #poetry
#amwriting #Billosophy
#gardensofEva

Sept. 12

Real, hyper-real, this moment,
heartbeat, breath, thought, vision, is
reality, all else history, memory,
imagination, fantasy, pour everything
into now, live here.

#ApoemAday #IAmEnough #poetry
#amwriting #Billosophy
#gardensofEva

Sept. 13

A life lived inside an epic novel
inspires the protagonist to commit
moments of each chapter to poetry.

#ApoemAday #IAmEnough #poetry
#amwriting #Billosophy
#gardensofEva

Sept. 14

Days shorten, darkness encroaches
on the afternoon, a chill lingers on
the horizon gently reminding of its
proximity, vegetables beckon to be
prepared and placed in jars, nap
time, a warm blanket awaits in a
closet.

#ApoemAday #IAmEnough #poetry
#amwriting #gardensofEva

Sept. 15

falling in love, too random, of life's
choices, choosing to love posts a
high ranking, with heart, mind, body
and soul aligned, choosing to love
rewards itself, from love I become
love.

#ApoemADay #IAmEnough #poetry
#amwriting #Billosophy
#gardensofEva

Sept. 16

lightness entirely fills my being, the universe vibrates my core, cosmic song stimulating DNA, move, keep moving, not running from, not running to, dancing, being fully, filling my skin, expanding into life, living.

#ApoemAday #gardensofEva #Billosophy #poetry #IAmEnough

Sept. 17

This moment, inhale, see, feel,
release the past, purposefully create
the future, fill the present with
presence.

#ApoemAday #IAmEnough #poetry
#amwriting #Billosophy
#gardensofEva

Sept. 18

When it all slips away, and I have no memory of day to day, will I remember it is you, when nothing else matters, will I remember love?

Sept. 19

When times are good, when times
are bad, there is something tangible
to grasp, there are times when there
is nothing, not floating, not falling,
excruciating nothingness, within the
nothing is time to conjure miracles.

Sept. 20

Time, ebbing flowing, moving too
fast, crawling to slow, projecting
illusions of past and future, changing
its skin in dream, remaining
constantly now.

Sept. 21

This is the moment, the epitome of now, the time before whatever and who knows, a moment to move or stay still, a moment lived to be remembered or forgotten, this is it and all there is.

#ApoemAday #IAmEnough #poetry #amwriting #Billosophy #gardensofEva

Sept. 22

Seamlessly the night before
becomes the day of, washing away
the previous self, the light of now
pouring through all, self becomes
clear, transparently divine.

#ApoemAday #IAmEnough #poetry
#amwriting #Billosophy
#gardensofEva

Sept. 23

love, unbinds, creating space, for
breath, for thought, reaction versus
response, gently holding the heart,
protected by the spirit, fully awake in
the dream state, allow possibilities to
generate form.

#APoemADay #IAmEnough #poetry
#amwriting #Billosophy
#gardensofEva

Sept. 24

The heart, powerful, unresting,
fragile and delicate, conflicted in
purpose by mind and spirit, only
capable of loving and healing.

#ApoemAday #IAmEnough #poetry
#amwriting #Billosophy
#gardensofEva

Sept. 25

The dream, a pebble on the shore of
the cosmic seas, a possibility to be
discovered, a lifetime to be lived, a
reality in extreme, to be lived once
the dreamer has been dreamed.

Sept. 26

the only thing certain is the
uncertainty, ups and downs lend to
the appreciation of the in between,
guided by mistakes, love happens, a
reassurance that the uncertainty has
rewards.

#ApoemAday #IAmEnough #poetry
#Billosophy #amwriting
#gardenofEva

Sept. 27

Gently push through the veil, pulling
the fantastic from the mind into the
now, dissolve the illusion, allow the
freedom of divine magical existence.

#ApoemAday #IAmEnough #poetry
#amwriting #Billosophy
#gardensofEva

Sept. 28

necessary and unseen, impossible to
be without, crucial to the heart's
franchise, and undetectable with
these eyes, life is lived with air and
love.

#ApoemAday #IAmEnough #poetry
#amwriting #Billosophy
#gardensofEva

Sept. 29

There are moments, sporadically
appearing, of nothing, no thought,
no sound, no desire, no fear, life
paused, the divine dance of nada, a
lifetime in a moment, the answer to
all prayer.

#ApoemAday #IAmEnough #poetry
#amwriting #Billosophy
#gardensofEva

Sept. 30

Go where there is no path, soar
when falling becomes unbearable,
sing when the voice is unheard, love
against all odds, far too often
foolishness is misunderstood faith.

About the author:

William Forchion brings his experience as a professional Clown, Acrobat, Stuntman and Voice performer to his thought provoking stream of consciousness writing. William is also a motivational speaker for corporate and academic audiences. William can also be found traveling the world with his solo theater show "Billosophy: life ~ circus ~ death". His Billosophy podcast can be heard at www.theearspoon.com You can find out more about William at www.billforchion.com.